D1339153

The World's Wife

Carol Ann Duffy lives in Manchester, where she is
Professor and Creative Director of the Writing School at
Manchester Metropolitan University. She has written for both
children and adults, and her poetry has received many awards,
including the Signal Prize for Children's Verse, the Whitbread
and Forward Prizes, and the Lannan and E. M. Forster Prize in
America. In 2005, she won the T. S. Eliot Prize for *Rapture*.
She was appointed Poet Laureate in 2009.In 2011
The Bees won the Costa Poetry Award, and
in 2012 she won the PEN Pinter Prize.
She was appointed DBE in 2015.

The World's Wife

CAROL ANN DUFFY

With an introduction by Jeanette Winterson

PICADOR CLASSIC

First published 1999 by Picador

First published in paperback 2000 by Picador

This Picador Classic edition first published 2015 by Picador
an imprint of Pan Macmillan
20 New Wharf Road, London N1 9RR
Associated companies throughout the world
www.panmacmillan.com

ISBN 978-1-4472-7524-4

3 5 7 9 8 6 4 2

A CIP catalogue record for this book is available from the British Library.

Typeset by SetSystems Limited, Saffron Walden, Essex
Printed and bound by CPI Group (UK) Ltd, Croydon, CR0 4YY

Visit **www.picador.com/classic** to read more about all our books
and to buy them. You will also find features, author interviews and
news of any author events, and you can sign up for e-newsletters
so that you're always first to hear about our new releases.

Introduction

Poetry is pleasure.

Sometimes people say to me, 'Why should I read a poem?' There are plenty of answers, from the profound – a poem is such an ancient means of communication that it feels like an evolutionary necessity – to the practical; a poem is like a shot of espresso – the fastest way to get a hit of mental and spiritual energy.

We could talk about poetry as a rope in a storm. Poetry as one continuous mantra of mental health. Poetry as the world's biggest, longest-running workshop on how to love. Poetry as a conversation across time. Poetry as the acid-scrub of cliché.

We could say that the poem is a lie-detector. That the poem is a way of thinking without losing the feeling. That a poem is a way of feeling without being too overwhelmed by feeling to think straight. That the poem is 'the best words in the best order' (Coleridge). That the poem 'keeps the heart awake to truth and beauty' (Coleridge again – who can resist those Romantics?).

That the poem is an intervention: 'The capacity to make change in existing conditions' (Muriel Rukeyser).

That poetry, said Seamus Heaney, is 'strong enough to help'.

Yes.

And pleasure.

Carol Ann Duffy has often spoken about poetry as an everyday event and not as a special occasion. She wants us to enjoy poetry, to have as much as we like, to be able to help ourselves to a good fresh supply, to let poetry be as daily as talking – because poetry is talking. Words begin in the mouth before they hit the page. Speech is older than writing and poetry is as old as speech. Poems are best spoken to get the full weight and taste of the words and the run of the lines. Difficult poems become easier when spoken.

Just as the body is shaped for movement, the mind is shaped for poetry.

Rhythm and rhyme aid recall. Poems are always rhythmic but not always rhyming. In the same way that melody became rather suspect in twentieth-century classical music – atonal fractures being the mark of seriousness – so Modernism re-branded rhyme as pastoral, lovesick, feminine, superficial.

Fine for kids and tea-towels, not fine for the muscular combative voice of the urban poet.

It has taken a long time for rhyme to return to favour. Rap, and the rise of performance poetry, has been part of that return.

As a powerful modern voice, Carol Ann Duffy has been unafraid to use rhyme from the beginning of her poetry ('Alphabet for Auden', *Standing Female Nude*, 1985). Twenty years later, in her quantum collection, *Rapture*, poem after poem deployed rhyme with accurate beauty.

Duffy's poetry is a practical proof of rhyme as expressive, flexible, purposefully baited. Dangle a rhyme at the end of a line and the mind-fish bites.

Not only end-rhymes, but off-rhymes, hidden rhymes, half-rhymes, ghost rhymes, deliberate near-misses that hit the mark:

> I was wind, I was gas
> I was all hot air, trailed
> clouds for hair.
> I scrawled my name with a hurricane,
> when out of the blue
> roared a fighter plane.
>
> (from 'Thetis')

The poems in *The World's Wife* are rhyme rich – not always obviously so:

> I flew in my chains over the wood where we'd buried
> the doll. I know it was me who was there.
> I know I carried the spade. I know I was covered in mud.
> But I cannot remember how or when or precisely where.

The complacent end-rhymes of lines 2 and 4 are taunted by the askew 'buried' and 'carried', and made sinister by the pagan sacrifice embedded in 'wood' and 'mud' with the ancient 'wude' and 'daub' sitting behind the rhyme.

Repetition of 'I know', three times in four lines, works as a locked rhyme – lethally right for a mind that can never escape itself or be set free by others; a mind that belongs to Myra Hindley.

Other poems rhyme with cheeky exuberance. 'Mrs Sisyphus', where the repetitive idiocy of the rock and its roll suits the uphill build of the poem (towards its inevitable collapse). The punishment of the gods turns out to be a 24/7 always-on meaningless managerial job, where no matter how many emails you answer, your inbox will be full again the next day.

Then there's the glorious five-line 'Mrs Darwin' with its Edward Lear nonsensical sense.

> 7 April 1852.
>
> Went to the Zoo.
> I said to Him –
> Something about that Chimpanzee over there reminds me
>   of you.

Hidden behind this ditty in diary form is the shadow of Dorothy Wordsworth, endlessly walking, endlessly writing her Lake District journal so that William could use it for that 'emotion recollected in tranquillity' he liked a poem to be. The famous daffodils, we remember, were Dorothy's.

Women behind the scenes, women behind the throne, women behind history, are the women figured in *The World's Wife* – the title itself both a tacit understanding that it's (still) a man's world, and a joke on the world's most popular dedication – To My Wife.

Ask who was at a party and the answer is often – oh, the world and his wife. Our language pictures are inherently patriarchal –

unless challenged. But the fact that three simple title-words can be the challenger affirms the power of language to disclose the unthought norm.

And the unthought known. Men and women alike know that more than half the world is female but men and women alike forget it every day. It takes a poet to jog our memory.

The characters in *The World's Wife* come out of fairy tales, Bible stories, legends, modern horrors (Myra Hindley, here re-cast as the Devil's Wife), and ancient myths. Their common link is that the poems themselves are told by the spouse-voice of the famous male.

This headstand, the world turned upside down, gives us another look at history through her-story. The 'other'; the angry and the ignored, as well as the sure-footed and sexy. Of course there's a political agenda – there always is – poets write poems because they have something urgent to say.

First World War poet and soldier Wilfred Owen claimed of his work that 'the poetry is in the pity.' In *The World's Wife*, the politics is in the poetry. The politics is feminism.

But there's nothing po-faced about these poems. They are written with such humour or poignancy, or insight or recognition, that we get the point, the many points, the points of view and the points of light. Like every good atom, these poems are composed out of empty space and points of lights – the dazzle of the poet's vision, the space for the reader to re-imagine matter, the matter, what matters, what is the matter?

Here is Frau Freud, in mad lexical delight, listing every word she can think of for Penis – and at last, in a bout of new theory-making that would have given us a very different psychoanalysis, she drops Penis Envy and opts instead for Penis Pity.

It's a short poem – a loose sonnet – but it says in its 14.1 lines as much as bookshelves of debate. The fact is that women don't suffer from penis envy. (Actually or symbolically, practically or poetically.) Only a man would think anyone could.

Here's Red Riding Hood gutting the wolf-poet to get at his words. She has no objection to sleeping with him first, or bringing him breakfast in bed. When she gets on with the axe-work and slits him, '*scrotum to throat*', she discovers it's her grandmother's bones inside. The skeleton of language is female. Deeper, it seems, than our mother tongue.

There's Mrs Midas, who has to lock the cat in the cellar and jam a chair against the bedroom door, while her husband turns their life into gold.

What you risk reveals what you value. This thoughtful, funny poem questions the masculine obsession with money – far from the stereotype of woman as a gold-digger. What Mrs Midas misses most about her husband is the one thing she can never have; his touch.

Mrs Faust draws up a much more money-minded female. It's Faust who has amassed world-pools of cash but she's happy enough to spend it.

> I grew to love the lifestyle,
> not the life.
> He grew to love the kudos,
> not the wife.

The ballad form rhyming here is tidy and deadly. Carol Ann Duffy, throughout her work, has made good use of both the English ballad and its nineteenth-century development, the dramatic monologue.

The ballad form is made for narrative stretch. It's an old form – the Robin Hood ballads are early fifteenth century. It's a form for storytelling, for late-night firesides, for pub entertainment, for the popular chapbooks (cheap books), that were just folded printed papers sold at fairs. It's street-corner, it's troubadour, it's busking.

Ballads had a lucrative disruptive sideline as political agitprop. Broadside ballads, as they became known.

In 1798, Wordsworth and Coleridge, the Lennon and McCartney of the eighteenth-century poetry scene, published their *Lyrical Ballads*, a moody, up-close, melodic extension of the ballad form, making it both personal and political – about ordinary people, not legends or hate-figures, and using natural speech and the sights and sounds of what was around them. They were modernizing poetry.

The ballad is usually a third-person narrative, and it can run on for ever – it was designed to have verses added – while its later development, the dramatic monologue, throws the reader into a highly charged first-person narrative, closer to the urgencies of the stage than the shaggy dog of a story.

But both forms have a story to tell.

The poems in *The World's Wife* are hybrids; first-person, dramatic situations, intimate and theatrical all at the same time, as you'd expect from a monologue, but with the authority of a ballad – a legend being told, a larger-than-life figure that belongs in myth as well as history. And there's something of the broadside here too, in their high-stepping protest at the truth that the story unfolds.

Some of these poems are laments for women in captivity.

The dramatic Mrs Beast pictures a world where smart women with their own money ditch the Prince and choose the Beast. Better sex. Keys to the wine cellar. The women run a weekly poker game

> But behind each player stood a line of ghosts
> unable to win. Eve. Ashputtel. Marilyn Monroe.
> Rapunzel wildly slashing at her hair.
> Bessie Smith unloved and down and out.
> Bluebeard's wives, Henry VIII's, Snow White
> cursing the day she left the seven dwarfs, Diana,
> Princess of Wales.

The startling last line of the poem? A paraphrase of Auden 'Let the less-loving one be me.'

From women who need a lesson in loving less to a creature who could not love more, 'Queen Kong' is the story of a female gorilla who falls in love with the documentary film-maker who turns up in her remote part of the world. They have an affair – he leaves for home, much like Aeneas leaves Dido, but this gorilla doesn't kill herself – she goes after him to New York city, squeezing herself between the skyscrapers,

> pressing my passionate eye
> to a thousand windows, each with its modest peep-show
> of boredom or pain, of drama, consolation, remorse.

Until . . .

> I picked him, like a chocolate from the top layer
> of a box, one Friday night, out of his room

It's a wonderful image, and as she dangles him there, high over the Manhattan grid, we get a new sense of what is meant by arm-candy.

The stanzas are seven-line riffs – half sonnets. Formal, held, but with the openness of the next verse – the ballad that continues, the monologue whose dialogue is with us – the reader.

The roaming range of Carol Ann Duffy's imagination is vast.

She moves easily from gorilla-scale to the interiority of the sonnet. Carol Ann Duffy loves the sonnet form – she says 'they remind me of prayers'.

'Anne Hathaway' is a sonnet – a gentle vindication of the love between the famously neglected wife of the most famous writer in history. For those who fear that feminism doesn't include men, except at the level of anger or contempt, read this one.

The final poem in the collection, 'Demeter', is a sonnet, as mysterious and complete as the moon.

The poem is about nobody's wife. That choice is an audacious signal. A message that something else is happening now. We are leaving for elsewhere. A new beginning.

'Demeter' celebrates mother and daughter in their ancient form as the two-that-is-three of the Great Goddess – mother, daughter, wise-woman. I guess the invisible third is writing the poem – or perhaps she's renewed, as she always is, in the new moon of the last line.

'Demeter' is a love poem. A poem of spring and the coming future; its symbol, fresh flowers. A future, perhaps, where there will be no need to voice history with the words we never heard.

A future that starts with a prayer.

Jeanette Winterson

for May and Jackie and Ella

with love

Acknowledgements

Some of these poems have previously appeared in *After Ovid* (ed. Hofmann and Lasdun, Faber, 1994); *The Big Issue*; *The Guardian*; *The New Statesman*; *The Pamphlet* (Anvil, 1998); *Poetry Review*; *Seven Deadly Sins* (Brighton Festival, 1998); *TLS*; or have been broadcast on BBC radio and television.

A huge acknowledgement, with love and thanks, is due to Brendan Kennelly.

Contents

The World's Wife

Little Red-Cap

At childhood's end, the houses petered out
into playing fields, the factory, allotments
kept, like mistresses, by kneeling married men,
the silent railway line, the hermit's caravan,
till you came at last to the edge of the woods.
It was there that I first clapped eyes on the wolf.

He stood in a clearing, reading his verse out loud
in his wolfy drawl, a paperback in his hairy paw,
red wine staining his bearded jaw. What big ears
he had! What big eyes he had! What teeth!
In the interval, I made quite sure he spotted me,
sweet sixteen, never been, babe, waif, and bought me a drink,

my first. You might ask why. Here's why. Poetry.
The wolf, I knew, would lead me deep into the woods,
away from home, to a dark tangled thorny place
lit by the eyes of owls. I crawled in his wake,
my stockings ripped to shreds, scraps of red from my blazer
snagged on twig and branch, murder clues. I lost both shoes

but got there, wolf's lair, better beware. Lesson one that
        night,
breath of the wolf in my ear, was the love poem.
I clung till dawn to his thrashing fur, for
what little girl doesn't dearly love a wolf?
Then I slid from between his heavy matted paws
and went in search of a living bird – white dove –

which flew, straight, from my hands to his open mouth.
One bite, dead. How nice, breakfast in bed, he said,
licking his chops. As soon as he slept, I crept to the back
of the lair, where a whole wall was crimson, gold, aglow with
     books.
Words, words were truly alive on the tongue, in the head,
warm, beating, frantic, winged; music and blood.

But then I was young – and it took ten years
in the woods to tell that a mushroom
stoppers the mouth of a buried corpse, that birds
are the uttered thought of trees, that a greying wolf
howls the same old song at the moon, year in, year out,
season after season, same rhyme, same reason. I took an axe

to a willow to see how it wept. I took an axe to a salmon
to see how it leapt. I took an axe to the wolf
as he slept, one chop, scrotum to throat, and saw
the glistening, virgin white of my grandmother's bones.
I filled his old belly with stones. I stitched him up.
Out of the forest I come with my flowers, singing, all alone.

Thetis

I shrank myself
to the size of a bird in the hand
of a man.
Sweet, sweet, was the small song
that I sang,
till I felt the squeeze of his fist.

Then I did this:
shouldered the cross of an albatross
up the hill of the sky.
Why? To follow a ship.
But I felt my wings
clipped by the squint of a crossbow's eye.

So I shopped for a suitable shape.
Size 8. Snake.
Big Mistake.
Coiled in my charmer's lap,
I felt the grasp of his strangler's clasp
at my nape.

Next I was roar, claw, 50 lb paw,
jungle-floored, meateater, raw,
a zebra's gore
in my lower jaw.
But my gold eye saw
the guy in the grass with the gun. Twelve-bore.

I sank through the floor of the earth
to swim in the sea.
Mermaid, me, big fish, eel, dolphin,
whale, the ocean's opera singer.
Over the waves the fisherman came
with his hook and his line and his sinker.

I changed my tune
to racoon, skunk, stoat,
to weasel, ferret, bat, mink, rat.
The taxidermist sharpened his knives.
I smelled the stink of formaldehyde.
Stuff that.

I was wind, I was gas,
I was all hot air, trailed
clouds for hair.
I scrawled my name with a hurricane,
when out of the blue
roared a fighter plane.

Then my tongue was flame
and my kisses burned,
but the groom wore asbestos.
So I changed, I learned,
turned inside out – or that's
how it felt when the child burst out.

Queen Herod

Ice in the trees.
Three Queens at the Palace gates,
dressed in furs, accented;
their several sweating, panting beasts,
laden for a long, hard trek,
following the guide and boy to the stables;
courteous, confident; oh, and with gifts
for the King and Queen of here – Herod, me –
in exchange for sunken baths, curtained beds,
fruit, the best of meat and wine,
dancers, music, talk –
as it turned out to be,
with everyone fast asleep, save me,
those vivid three –
till bitter dawn.

They were wise. Older than I.
They knew what they knew.
Once drunken Herod's head went back,
they asked to see her,
fast asleep in her crib,
my little child.
Silver and gold,
the loose change of herself,
glowed in the soft bowl of her face.
Grace, said the tallest Queen.
Strength, said the Queen with the hennaed hands.
The black Queen
made a tiny starfish of my daughter's fist,
said *Happiness*; then stared at me,
Queen to Queen, with insolent lust.
Watch, they said, *for a star in the East –*
a new star
pierced through the night like a nail.
It means he's here, alive, new-born.
Who? *Him. The Husband. Hero. Hunk.*
The Boy Next Door. The Paramour. The Je t'adore.
The Marrying Kind. Adulterer. Bigamist.
The Wolf. The Rip. The Rake. The Rat.
The Heartbreaker. The Ladykiller. Mr Right.

My baby stirred,
suckled the empty air for milk,
till I knelt
and the black Queen scooped out my breast,
the left, guiding it down
to the infant's mouth.
No man, I swore,
will make her shed one tear.
A peacock screamed outside.

Afterwards, it seemed like a dream.
The pungent camels
kneeling in the snow,
the guide's rough shout
as he clapped his leather gloves,
hawked, spat, snatched
the smoky jug of mead
from the chittering maid –
she was twelve, thirteen.
I watched each turbaned Queen
rise like a god on the back of her beast.
And splayed that night
below Herod's fusty bulk,
I saw the fierce eyes of the black Queen
flash again, felt her urgent warnings scald
my ear. *Watch for a star, a star.*
It means he's here . . .

Some swaggering lad to break her heart,
some wincing Prince to take her name away
and give a ring, a nothing, nowt in gold.
I sent for the Chief of Staff,
a mountain man
with a red scar, like a tick
to the mean stare of his eye.
Take men and horses,
knives, swords, cutlasses.
Ride East from here
and kill each mother's son.
Do it. Spare not one.

The midnight hour. The chattering stars
shivered in a nervous sky.
Orion to the South
who knew the score, who'd seen,
not seen, then seen it all before;
the yapping Dog Star at his heels.
High up in the West
a studded, diamond W.
And then, as prophesied,
blatant, brazen, buoyant in the East –
and blue –
The Boyfriend's Star.

We do our best,
we Queens, we mothers,
mothers of Queens.

We wade through blood
for our sleeping girls.
We have daggers for eyes.

Behind our lullabies,
the hooves of terrible horses
thunder and drum.

Mrs Midas

It was late September. I'd just poured a glass of wine, begun
to unwind, while the vegetables cooked. The kitchen
filled with the smell of itself, relaxed, its steamy breath
gently blanching the windows. So I opened one,
then with my fingers wiped the other's glass like a brow.
He was standing under the pear tree snapping a twig.

Now the garden was long and the visibility poor, the way
the dark of the ground seems to drink the light of the sky,
but that twig in his hand was gold. And then he plucked
a pear from a branch – we grew Fondante d'Automne –
and it sat in his palm like a light bulb. On.
I thought to myself, Is he putting fairy lights in the tree?

He came into the house. The doorknobs gleamed.
He drew the blinds. You know the mind; I thought of
the Field of the Cloth of Gold and of Miss Macready.
He sat in that chair like a king on a burnished throne.
The look on his face was strange, wild, vain. I said,
What in the name of God is going on? He started to laugh.

I served up the meal. For starters, corn on the cob.
Within seconds he was spitting out the teeth of the rich.
He toyed with his spoon, then mine, then with the knives, the
        forks.
He asked where was the wine. I poured with a shaking hand,
a fragrant, bone-dry white from Italy, then watched
as he picked up the glass, goblet, golden chalice, drank.

It was then that I started to scream. He sank to his knees.
After we'd both calmed down, I finished the wine
on my own, hearing him out. I made him sit
on the other side of the room and keep his hands to himself.
I locked the cat in the cellar. I moved the phone.
The toilet I didn't mind. I couldn't believe my ears:

how he'd had a wish. Look, we all have wishes; granted.
But who has wishes granted? Him. Do you know about gold?
It feeds no one; aurum, soft, untarnishable; slakes
no thirst. He tried to light a cigarette; I gazed, entranced,
as the blue flame played on its luteous stem. At least,
I said, you'll be able to give up smoking for good.

Separate beds. In fact, I put a chair against my door,
near petrified. He was below, turning the spare room
into the tomb of Tutankhamun. You see, we were passionate
        then,
in those halcyon days; unwrapping each other, rapidly,
like presents, fast food. But now I feared his honeyed
        embrace,
the kiss that would turn my lips to a work of art.

And who, when it comes to the crunch, can live
with a heart of gold? That night, I dreamt I bore
his child, its perfect ore limbs, its little tongue
like a precious latch, its amber eyes
holding their pupils like flies. My dream-milk
burned in my breasts. I woke to the streaming sun.

So he had to move out. We'd a caravan
in the wilds, in a glade of its own. I drove him up
under cover of dark. He sat in the back.
And then I came home, the woman who married the fool
who wished for gold. At first I visited, odd times,
parking the car a good way off, then walking.

You knew you were getting close. Golden trout
on the grass. One day, a hare hung from a larch,
a beautiful lemon mistake. And then his footprints,
glistening next to the river's path. He was thin,
delirious; hearing, he said, the music of Pan
from the woods. Listen. That was the last straw.

What gets me now is not the idiocy or greed
but lack of thought for me. Pure selfishness. I sold
the contents of the house and came down here.
I think of him in certain lights, dawn, late afternoon,
and once a bowl of apples stopped me dead. I miss most,
even now, his hands, his warm hands on my skin, his touch.

from Mrs Tiresias

All I know is this:
he went out for his walk a man
and came home female.

Out the back gate with his stick,
the dog;
wearing his gardening kecks,
an open-necked shirt,
and a jacket in Harris tweed I'd patched at the elbows myself.

Whistling.

He liked to hear
the first cuckoo of spring
then write to *The Times*.
I'd usually heard it
days before him
but I never let on.

I'd heard one that morning
while he was asleep;
just as I heard,
at about 6 p.m.,
a faint sneer of thunder up in the woods
and felt
a sudden heat
at the back of my knees.

He was late getting back.

I was brushing my hair at the mirror
and running a bath
when a face
swam into view
next to my own.

The eyes were the same.
But in the shocking V of the shirt were breasts.
When he uttered my name in his woman's voice I passed out.

*

Life has to go on.

I put it about that he was a twin
and this was his sister
come down to live
while he himself
was working abroad.

And at first I tried to be kind;
blow-drying his hair till he learnt to do it himself,
lending him clothes till he started to shop for his own,
sisterly, holding his soft new shape in my arms all night.

Then he started his period.

One week in bed.
Two doctors in.
Three painkillers four times a day.

And later
a letter
to the powers that be
demanding full-paid menstrual leave twelve weeks per year.
I see him still,
his selfish pale face peering at the moon
through the bathroom window.
The curse, he said, *the curse.*

Don't kiss me in public,
he snapped the next day,
I don't want folk getting the wrong idea.

It got worse.

*

After the split I would glimpse him
out and about,
entering glitzy restaurants
on the arms of powerful men –
though I knew for sure
there'd be nothing of *that*
going on
if he had his way –
or on TV
telling the women out there
how, as a woman himself,
he knew how we felt.

His flirt's smile.

The one thing he never got right
was the voice.
A cling peach slithering out from its tin.

I gritted my teeth.

*

And this is my lover, I said,
the one time we met
at a glittering ball
under the lights,
among tinkling glass,
and watched the way he stared
at her violet eyes,
at the blaze of her skin,
at the slow caress of her hand on the back of my neck;
and saw him picture
her bite,
her bite at the fruit of my lips,
and hear
my red wet cry in the night
as she shook his hand
saying *How do you do*;
and I noticed then his hands, her hands,
the clash of their sparkling rings and their painted nails.

Pilate's Wife

Firstly, his hands – a woman's. Softer than mine,
with pearly nails, like shells from Galilee.
Indolent hands. Camp hands that clapped for grapes.
Their pale, mothy touch made me flinch. Pontius.

I longed for Rome, home, someone else. When the Nazarene
entered Jerusalem, my maid and I crept out,
bored stiff, disguised, and joined the frenzied crowd.
I tripped, clutched the bridle of an ass, looked up

and there he was. His face? Ugly. Talented.
He looked at me. I mean he looked at *me*. My God.
His eyes were eyes to die for. Then he was gone,
his rough men shouldering a pathway to the gates.

The night before his trial, I dreamt of him.
His brown hands touched me. Then it hurt.
Then blood. I saw that each tough palm was skewered
by a nail. I woke up, sweating, sexual, terrified.

Leave him alone. I sent a warning note, then quickly dressed.
When I arrived, the Nazarene was crowned with thorns.
The crowd was baying for Barabbas. Pilate saw me,
looked away, then carefully turned up his sleeves

and slowly washed his useless, perfumed hands.
They seized the prophet then and dragged him out,
up to the Place of Skulls. My maid knows all the rest.
Was he God? Of course not. Pilate believed he was.

Mrs Aesop

By Christ, he could bore for Purgatory. He was small,
didn't prepossess. So he tried to impress. *Dead men,*
Mrs Aesop, he'd say, *tell no tales.* Well, let me tell you now
that the bird in his hand shat on his sleeve,
never mind the two worth less in the bush. Tedious.

Going out was worst. He'd stand at our gate, look, then leap;
scour the hedgerows for a shy mouse, the fields
for a sly fox, the sky for one particular swallow
that couldn't make a summer. The jackdaw, according to
      him,
envied the eagle. Donkeys would, on the whole, prefer to be
      lions.

On one appalling evening stroll, we passed an old hare
snoozing in a ditch – he stopped and made a note –
and then, about a mile further on, a tortoise, somebody's pet,
creeping, slow as marriage, up the road. *Slow*
but certain, Mrs Aesop, wins the race. Asshole.

What race? What sour grapes? What silk purse,
sow's ear, dog in a manger, what big fish? Some days
I could barely keep awake as the story droned on
towards the moral of itself. *Action, Mrs A., speaks louder*
than words. And that's another thing, the sex

was diabolical. I gave him a fable one night
about a little cock that wouldn't crow, a razor-sharp axe
with a heart blacker than the pot that called the kettle.
I'll cut off your tail, all right, I said, *to save my face.*
That shut him up. I laughed last, longest.

Mrs Darwin

7 April 1852.

Went to the Zoo.
I said to Him –
Something about that Chimpanzee over there reminds me of
    you.

Mrs Sisyphus

That's him pushing the stone up the hill, the jerk.
I call it a stone – it's nearer the size of a kirk.
When he first started out, it just used to irk,
but now it incenses me, and him, the absolute berk.
I could do something vicious to him with a dirk.

Think of the perks, he says.
What use is a perk, I shriek,
when you haven't the time to pop open a cork
or go for so much as a walk in the park?
He's a dork.
Folk flock from miles around just to gawk.
They think it's a quirk,
a bit of a lark.
A load of old bollocks is nearer the mark.
He might as well bark
at the moon –
that feckin' stone's no sooner up
than it's rolling back
all the way down.
And what does he say?
Mustn't shirk –
keen as a hawk,
lean as a shark
Mustn't shirk!

But I lie alone in the dark,
feeling like Noah's wife did
when he hammered away at the Ark;
like Frau Johann Sebastian Bach.
My voice reduced to a squawk,
my smile to a twisted smirk;
while, up on the deepening murk of the hill,
he is giving one hundred per cent and more to his work.

Mrs Faust

First things first –
I married Faust.
We met as students,
shacked up, split up,
made up, hitched up,
got a mortgage on a house,
flourished academically,
BA. MA. Ph.D. No kids.
Two towelled bathrobes. Hers. His.

We worked. We saved.
We moved again.
Fast cars. A boat with sails.
A second home in Wales.
The latest toys – computers,
mobile phones. Prospered.
Moved again. Faust's face
was clever, greedy, slightly mad.
I was as bad.

I grew to love the lifestyle,
not the life.
He grew to love the kudos,
not the wife.
He went to whores.
I felt, not jealousy,
but chronic irritation.
I went to yoga, t'ai chi,
Feng Shui, therapy, colonic irrigation.

And Faust would boast
at dinner parties
of the cost
of doing deals out East.
Then take his lust
to Soho in a cab,
to say the least,
to lay the ghost,
get lost, meet panthers, feast.

He wanted more.
I came home late one winter's evening,
hadn't eaten.
Faust was upstairs in his study,
in a meeting.
I smelled cigar smoke,
hellish, oddly sexy, not allowed.
I heard Faust and the other
laugh aloud.

Next thing, the world,
as Faust said,
spread its legs.
First politics –
Safe seat. MP. Right Hon. KG.
Then banks –
offshore, abroad –
and business –
Vice-chairman. Chairman. Owner. Lord.

Enough? *Encore!*
Faust was Cardinal, Pope,
knew more than God;
flew faster than the speed of sound
around the globe,
lunched;
walked on the moon,
golfed, holed in one;
lit a fat Havana on the sun.

Then backed a hunch –
invested in smart bombs,
in harms,
Faust dealt in arms.
Faust got in deep, got out.
Bought farms,
cloned sheep,
Faust surfed the Internet
for like-minded Bo-Peep.

As for me,
I went my own sweet way,
saw Rome in a day,
spun gold from hay,
had a facelift,
had my breasts enlarged,
my buttocks tightened;
went to China, Thailand, Africa,
returned, enlightened.

Turned 40, celibate,
teetotal, vegan,
Buddhist, 41.
Went blonde,
redhead, brunette,
went native, ape,
berserk, bananas;
went on the run, alone;
went home.

Faust was in. *A word,* he said,
I spent the night being pleasured
by a virtual Helen of Troy.
Face that launched a thousand ships.
I kissed its lips.
Thing is –
I've made a pact
with Mephistopheles,
the Devil's boy.

He's on his way
to take away
what's owed,
reap what I sowed.
For all these years of
gagging for it,
going for it,
rolling in it,
I've sold my soul.

At this, I heard
a serpent's hiss,
tasted evil, knew its smell,
as scaly devil hands
poked up
right through the terracotta Tuscan tiles
at Faust's bare feet
and dragged him, oddly smirking, there and then
straight down to Hell.

Oh, well.
Faust's will
left everything –
the yacht,
the several homes,
the Lear jet, the helipad,
the loot, et cet, et cet,
the lot –
to me.

C'est la vie.
When I got ill,
it hurt like hell.
I bought a kidney
with my credit card,
then I got well.
I keep Faust's secret still –
the clever, cunning, callous bastard
didn't have a soul to sell.

Delilah

Teach me, he said –
we were lying in bed –
how to care.
I nibbled the purse of his ear.
What do you mean? Tell me more.
He sat up and reached for his beer.

I can rip out the roar
from the throat of a tiger,
or gargle with fire,
or sleep one whole night in the Minotaur's lair,
or flay the bellowing fur
from a bear,
all for a dare.
There's nothing I fear.
Put your hand here –

he guided my fingers over the scar
over his heart,
a four-medal wound from the war –
but I cannot be gentle, or loving, or tender.
I have to be strong.
What is the cure?

He fucked me again
until he was sore,
then we both took a shower.
Then he lay with his head on my lap
for a darkening hour;
his voice, for a change, a soft burr
I could just about hear.
And, yes, I was sure
that he wanted to change,
my warrior.

I was there.

So when I felt him soften and sleep,
when he started, as usual, to snore,
I let him slip and slide and sprawl, handsome and huge,
on the floor.
And before I fetched and sharpened my scissors –
snipping first at the black and biblical air –
I fastened the chain to the door.

That's the how and the why and the where.

Then with deliberate, passionate hands
I cut every lock of his hair.

Anne Hathaway

'Item I gyve unto my wief my second best bed . . .'
(from Shakespeare's will)

The bed we loved in was a spinning world
of forests, castles, torchlight, clifftops, seas
where he would dive for pearls. My lover's words
were shooting stars which fell to earth as kisses
on these lips; my body now a softer rhyme
to his, now echo, assonance; his touch
a verb dancing in the centre of a noun.
Some nights, I dreamed he'd written me, the bed
a page beneath his writer's hands. Romance
and drama played by touch, by scent, by taste.
In the other bed, the best, our guests dozed on,
dribbling their prose. My living laughing love –
I hold him in the casket of my widow's head
as he held me upon that next best bed.

Queen Kong

I remember peeping in at his skyscraper room
and seeing him fast asleep. My little man.
I'd been in Manhattan a week,
making my plans; staying at 2 quiet hotels
in the Village, where people were used to strangers
and more or less left you alone. To this day
I'm especially fond of pastrami on rye.

I digress. As you see, this island's a paradise.
He'd arrived, my man, with a documentary team
to make a film. (There's a particular toad
that lays its eggs only here.) I found him alone
in a clearing, scooped him up in my palm,
and held his wriggling, shouting life till he calmed.
For me, it was absolutely love at first sight.

I'd been so *lonely*. Long nights in the heat
of my own pelt, rumbling an animal blues.
All right, he was small, but perfectly formed
and *gorgeous*. There were things he could do
for me with the sweet finesse of those hands
that no gorilla could. I swore in my huge heart
to follow him then to the ends of the earth.

For he wouldn't stay here. He was nervous.
I'd go to his camp each night at dusk,
crouch by the delicate tents, and wait. His colleagues
always sent him out pretty quick. He'd climb
into my open hand, sit down; and then I'd gently pick
at his shirt and his trews, peel him, put
the tip of my tongue to the grape of his flesh.

Bliss. But when he'd finished his prize-winning film,
he packed his case; hopped up and down
on my heartline, miming the flight back home
to New York. *Big metal bird.* Didn't he know
I could swat his plane from these skies like a gnat?
But I let him go, my man. I watched him fly
into the sun as I thumped at my breast, distraught.

I lasted a month. I slept for a week,
then woke to binge for a fortnight. I didn't wash.
The parrots clacked their migraine chant.
The swinging monkeys whinged. Fevered, I drank
handfuls of river right by the spot where he'd bathed.
I bled when a fat, red moon rolled on the jungle roof.
And after that, I decided to get him back.

So I came to sail up the Hudson one June night,
with the New York skyline a concrete rainforest
of light; and felt, lovesick and vast, the first
glimmer of hope in weeks. I was discreet, prowled
those streets in darkness, pressing my passionate eye
to a thousand windows, each with its modest peep-show
of boredom or pain, of drama, consolation, remorse.

I found him, of course. At 3 a.m. on a Sunday,
dreaming alone in his single bed; over his lovely head
a blown-up photograph of myself. I stared for a long time
till my big brown eyes grew moist; then I padded away
through Central Park, under the stars. He was mine.
Next day, I shopped. Clothes for my man, mainly,
but one or two treats for myself from Bloomingdale's.

I picked him, like a chocolate from the top layer
of a box, one Friday night, out of his room
and let him dangle in the air betwen my finger
and my thumb in a teasing, lover's way. Then we sat
on the tip of the Empire State Building, saying farewell
to the Brooklyn Bridge, to the winking yellow cabs,
to the helicopters over the river, dragonflies.

Twelve happy years. He slept in my fur, woke early
to massage the heavy lids of my eyes. I liked that.
He liked me to gently blow on him; or scratch,
with care, the length of his back with my nail.
Then I'd ask him to play on the wooden pipes he'd made
in our first year. He'd sit, cross-legged, near my ear
for hours: his plaintive, lost tunes making me cry.

When he died, I held him all night, shaking him
like a doll, licking his face, breast, soles of his feet,
his little rod. But then, heartsore as I was, I set to work.
He would be pleased. I wear him now about my neck,
perfect, preserved, with tiny emeralds for eyes. No man
has been loved more. I'm sure that, sometimes, in his silent
        death,
against my massive, breathing lungs, he hears me roar.

Mrs Quasimodo

I'd loved them fervently since childhood.
Their generous bronze throats
gargling, or chanting slowly, calming me –
the village runt, name-called, stunted, lame, hare-lipped;
but bearing up, despite it all, sweet-tempered, good at
     needlework;
an ugly cliché in a field
pressing dock-leaves to her fat, stung calves
and listening to the five cool bells of evensong.
I believed that they could even make it rain.

The city suited me; my lumpy shadow
lurching on its jagged alley walls;
my small eyes black
as rained-on cobblestones.
I frightened cats.
I lived alone up seven flights,
boiled potatoes on a ring
and fried a single silver fish;
then stared across the grey lead roofs
as dusk's blue rubber rubbed them out,
and then the bells began.

I climbed the belltower steps,
out of breath and sweating anxiously, puce-faced,
and found the campanologists beneath their ropes.
They made a space for me,
telling their names,
and when it came to him
I felt a thump of confidence,
a recognition like a struck match in my head.
It was Christmas time.
When the others left,
he fucked me underneath the gaping, stricken bells
until I wept.

We wed.
He swung an epithalamium for me,
embossed it on the fragrant air.
Long, sexy chimes,
exuberant peals,
slow scales trailing up and down the smaller bells,
an angelus.
We had no honeymoon
but spent the week in bed.
And did I kiss
each part of him –
that horseshoe mouth,
that tetrahedron nose,
that squint left eye,
that right eye with its pirate wart,
the salty leather of that pig's hide throat,
and give his cock
a private name –
or not?

So more fool me.

We lived in the Cathedral grounds.
The bellringer.
The hunchback's wife.
(The Quasimodos. Have you met them? Gross.)
And got a life.
Our neighbours – sullen gargoyles, fallen angels, cowled
       saints
who raised their marble hands in greeting
as I passed along the gravel paths,
my husband's supper on a tray beneath a cloth.
But once,
one evening in the lady chapel on my own,
throughout his ringing of the seventh hour,
I kissed the cold lips of a Queen next to her King.

Something had changed,
or never been.
Soon enough
he started to find fault.
Why did I this?
How could I that?
Look at myself.
And in that summer's dregs,
I'd see him
watch the pin-up gypsy
posing with the tourists in the square;
then turn his discontented, mulish eye on me
with no more love than stone.

I should have known.

Because it's better, isn't it, to be well formed.
Better to be slim, be slight,
your slender neck quoted between two thumbs;
and beautiful, with creamy skin,
and tumbling auburn hair,
those devastating eyes;
and have each lovely foot
held in a bigger hand
and kissed;
then be watched till morning as you sleep,
so perfect, vulnerable and young
you hurt his blood.

And given sanctuary.

But not betrayed.
Not driven to an ecstasy of loathing of yourself:
banging your ugly head against a wall,
gaping in the mirror at your heavy dugs,
your thighs of lard,
your mottled upper arms;
thumping your belly –
look at it –
your wobbling gut.
You pig. You stupid cow. You fucking buffalo.
Abortion. Cripple. Spastic. Mongol. Ape.

Where did it end?
A ladder. Heavy tools. A steady hand.
And me, alone all night up there,
bent on revenge.
He had pet names for them.
Marie.
The belfry trembled when she spoke for him.
I climbed inside her with my claw-hammer,
my pliers, my saw, my clamp;
and, though it took an agonizing hour,
ripped out her brazen tongue
and let it fall.
Then Josephine,
his second-favourite bell,
kept open her astonished, golden lips
and let me in.
The bells. The bells.
I made them mute.
No more arpeggios or scales, no stretti, trills
for christenings, weddings, great occasions, happy days.
No more practising
for bellringers
on smudgy autumn nights.
No clarity of sound, divine, articulate,
to purify the air
and bow the heads of drinkers in the city bars.
No single
solemn
funeral note
to answer
grief.

I sawed and pulled and hacked.
I wanted silence back.

Get this:

When I was done,
and bloody to the wrist,
I squatted down among the murdered music of the bells
and pissed.

Medusa

A suspicion, a doubt, a jealousy
grew in my mind,
which turned the hairs on my head to filthy snakes,
as though my thoughts
hissed and spat on my scalp.

My bride's breath soured, stank
in the grey bags of my lungs.
I'm foul mouthed now, foul tongued,
yellow fanged.
There are bullet tears in my eyes.
Are you terrified?

Be terrified.
It's you I love,
perfect man, Greek God, my own;
but I know you'll go, betray me, stray
from home.
So better by far for me if you were stone.

I glanced at a buzzing bee,
a dull grey pebble fell
to the ground.
I glanced at a singing bird,
a handful of dusty gravel
spattered down.

I looked at a ginger cat,
a housebrick
shattered a bowl of milk.
I looked at a snuffling pig,
a boulder rolled
in a heap of shit.

I stared in the mirror.
Love gone bad
showed me a Gorgon.
I stared at a dragon.
Fire spewed
from the mouth of a mountain.

And here you come
with a shield for a heart
and a sword for a tongue
and your girls, your girls.
Wasn't I beautiful?
Wasn't I fragrant and young?

Look at me now.

The Devil's Wife

The Devil was one of the men at work.
Different. Fancied himself. Looked at the girls
in the office as though they were dirt. Didn't flirt.
Didn't speak. Was sarcastic and rude if he did.
I'd stare him out, chewing my gum, insolent, dumb.
I'd lie on my bed at home, on fire for him.

I scowled and pouted and sneered. I gave
as good as I got till he asked me out. In his car
he put two fags in his mouth and lit them both.
He bit my breast. His language was foul. He entered me.
We're the same, he said, That's it. I swooned in my soul.
We drove to the woods and he made me bury a doll.

I went mad for the sex. I won't repeat what we did.
We gave up going to work. It was either the woods
or looking at playgrounds, fairgrounds. Coloured lights
in the rain. I'd walk around on my own. He tailed.
I felt like this: Tongue of stone. Two black slates
for eyes. Thumped wound of a mouth. Nobody's Mam.

2. MEDUSA

I flew in my chains over the wood where we'd buried
the doll. I know it was me who was there.
I know I carried the spade. I know I was covered in mud.
But I cannot remember how or when or precisely where.

Nobody liked my hair. Nobody liked how I spoke.
He held my heart in his fist and he squeezed it dry.
I gave the cameras my Medusa stare.
I heard the judge summing up. I didn't care.

I was left to rot. I was locked up, double-locked.
I know they chucked the key. It was nowt to me.
I wrote to him every day in our private code.
I thought in twelve, fifteen, we'd be out on the open road.

But life, they said, means life. Dying inside.
The Devil was evil, mad, but I was the Devil's wife
which made me worse. I howled in my cell.
If the Devil was gone then how could this be hell?

3 . BIBLE

I said No not me I didn't I couldn't I wouldn't.
Can't remember no idea not in the room.
Get me a Bible honestly promise you swear.
I never not in a million years it was him.

I said Send me a lawyer a vicar a priest.
Send me a TV crew send me a journalist.
Can't remember not in the room. Send me
a shrink where's my MP send him to me.

I said Not fair not right not on not true
not like that. Didn't see didn't know didn't hear.
Maybe this maybe that not sure not certain maybe.
Can't remember no idea it was him it was him.

Can't remember no idea not in the room.
No idea can't remember not in the room.

4. Night

In the long fifty-year night,
these are the words that crawl out of the wall:
Suffer. Monster. Burn in Hell.

When morning comes,
I will finally tell.

Amen.

5. APPEAL

If I'd been stoned to death
If I'd been hung by the neck
If I'd been shaved and strapped to the Chair
If an injection
If my peroxide head on the block
If my outstretched hands for the chop
If my tongue torn out at the root
If from ear to ear my throat
If a bullet a hammer a knife
If life means life means life means life

But what did I do to us all, to myself
When I was the Devil's wife?

Circe

I'm fond, nereids and nymphs, unlike some, of the pig,
of the tusker, the snout, the boar and the swine.
One way or another, all pigs have been mine –
under my thumb, the bristling, salty skin of their backs,
in my nostrils here, their yobby, porky colognes.
I'm familiar with hogs and runts, their percussion of oinks
and grunts, their squeals. I've stood with a pail of swill
at dusk, at the creaky gate of the sty,
tasting the sweaty, spicy air, the moon
like a lemon popped in the mouth of the sky.
But I want to begin with a recipe from abroad

which uses the cheek – and the tongue in cheek
at that. Lay two pig's cheeks, with the tongue,
in a dish, and strew it well over with salt
and cloves. Remember the skills of the tongue –
to lick, to lap, to loosen, lubricate, to lie
in the soft pouch of the face – and how each pig's face
was uniquely itself, as many handsome as plain,
the cowardly face, the brave, the comical, noble,
sly or wise, the cruel, the kind, but all of them,
nymphs, with those piggy eyes. Season with mace.

Well-cleaned pig's ears should be blanched, singed, tossed
in a pot, boiled, kept hot, scraped, served, garnished
with thyme. Look at that simmering lug, at that ear,
did it listen, ever, to you, to your prayers and rhymes,
to the chimes of your voice, singing and clear? Mash
the potatoes, nymph, open the beer. Now to the brains,
to the trotters, shoulders, chops, to the sweetmeats slipped
from the slit, bulging, vulnerable bag of the balls.
When the heart of a pig has hardened, dice it small.

Dice it small. I, too, once knelt on this shining shore
watching the tall ships sail from the burning sun
like myths; slipped off my dress to wade,
breast-deep, in the sea, waving and calling;
then plunged, then swam on my back, looking up
as three black ships sighed in the shallow waves.
Of course, I was younger then. And hoping for men. Now,
let us baste that sizzling pig on the spit once again.

Mrs Lazarus

I had grieved. I had wept for a night and a day
over my loss, ripped the cloth I was married in
from my breasts, howled, shrieked, clawed
at the burial stones till my hands bled, retched
his name over and over again, dead, dead.

Gone home. Gutted the place. Slept in a single cot,
widow, one empty glove, white femur
in the dust, half. Stuffed dark suits
into black bags, shuffled in a dead man's shoes,
noosed the double knot of a tie round my bare neck,

gaunt nun in the mirror, touching herself. I learnt
the Stations of Bereavement, the icon of my face
in each bleak frame; but all those months
he was going away from me, dwindling
to the shrunk size of a snapshot, going,

going. Till his name was no longer a certain spell
for his face. The last hair on his head
floated out from a book. His scent went from the house.
The will was read. See, he was vanishing
to the small zero held by the gold of my ring.

Then he was gone. Then he was legend, language;
my arm on the arm of the schoolteacher – the shock
of a man's strength under the sleeve of his coat –
along the hedgerows. But I was faithful
for as long as it took. Until he was memory.

So I could stand that evening in the field
in a shawl of fine air, healed, able
to watch the edge of the moon occur to the sky
and a hare thump from a hedge; then notice
the village men running towards me, shouting,

behind them the women and children, barking dogs,
and I knew. I knew by the sly light
on the blacksmith's face, the shrill eyes
of the barmaid, the sudden hands bearing me
into the hot tang of the crowd parting before me.

He lived. I saw the horror on his face.
I heard his mother's crazy song. I breathed
his stench; my bridegroom in his rotting shroud,
moist and dishevelled from the grave's slack chew,
croaking his cuckold name, disinherited, out of his time.

Pygmalion's Bride

Cold, I was, like snow, like ivory.
I thought *He will not touch me*,
but he did.

He kissed my stone-cool lips.
I lay still
as though I'd died.
He stayed.
He thumbed my marbled eyes.

He spoke –
blunt endearments, what he'd do and how.
His words were terrible.
My ears were sculpture,
stone-deaf, shells.
I heard the sea.
I drowned him out.
I heard him shout.

He brought me presents, polished pebbles,
little bells.
I didn't blink,
was dumb.
He brought me pearls and necklaces and rings.
He called them *girly things*.
He ran his clammy hands along my limbs.
I didn't shrink,
played statue, shtum.

He let his fingers sink into my flesh,
he squeezed, he pressed.
I would not bruise.
He looked for marks,
for purple hearts,
for inky stars, for smudgy clues.
His nails were claws.
I showed no scratch, no scrape, no scar.
He propped me up on pillows,
jawed all night.
My heart was ice, was glass.
His voice was gravel, hoarse.
He talked white black.

So I changed tack,
grew warm, like candle wax,
kissed back,
was soft, was pliable,
began to moan,
got hot, got wild,
arched, coiled, writhed,
begged for his child,
and at the climax
screamed my head off –
all an act.

And haven't seen him since.
Simple as that.

Mrs Rip Van Winkle

I sank like a stone
into the still, deep waters of late middle age,
aching from head to foot.

I took up food
and gave up exercise.
It did me good.

And while he slept
I found some hobbies for myself.
Painting. Seeing the sights I'd always dreamed about:

The Leaning Tower.
The Pyramids. The Taj Mahal.
I made a little watercolour of them all.

But what was best,
what hands-down beat the rest,
was saying a none-too-fond farewell to sex.

Until the day
I came home with this pastel of Niagara
and he was sitting up in bed rattling Viagra.

Mrs Icarus

I'm not the first or the last
to stand on a hillock,
watching the man she married
prove to the world
he's a total, utter, absolute, Grade A pillock.

Frau Freud

Ladies, for argument's sake, let us say
that I've seen my fair share of ding-a-ling, member and jock,
of todger and nudger and percy and cock, of tackle,
of three-for-a-bob, of willy and winky; in fact,
you could say, I'm as au fait with Hunt-the-Salami
as Ms M. Lewinsky – equally sick up to here
with the beef bayonet, the pork sword, the saveloy,
love-muscle, night-crawler, dong, the dick, prick,
dipstick and wick, the rammer, the slammer, the rupert,
the shlong. Don't get me wrong, I've no axe to grind
with the snake in the trousers, the wife's best friend,
the weapon, the python – I suppose what I mean is,
ladies, dear ladies, the average penis – not pretty . . .
the squint of its envious solitary eye . . . one's feeling of
      pity . . .

Salome

I'd done it before
(and doubtless I'll do it again,
sooner or later)
woke up with a head on the pillow beside me – whose? –
what did it matter?
Good-looking, of course, dark hair, rather matted;
the reddish beard several shades lighter;
with very deep lines round the eyes,
from pain, I'd guess, maybe laughter;
and a beautiful crimson mouth that obviously knew
how to flatter . . .
which I kissed . . .
Colder than pewter.
Strange. What was his name? Peter?

Simon? Andrew? John? I knew I'd feel better
for tea, dry toast, no butter,
so rang for the maid.
And, indeed, her innocent clatter
of cups and plates,
her clearing of clutter,
her regional patter,
were just what I needed –
hungover and wrecked as I was from a night on the batter.

Never again!
I needed to clean up my act,
get fitter,
cut out the booze and the fags and the sex.
Yes. And as for the latter,
it was time to turf out the blighter,
the beater or biter,
who'd come like a lamb to the slaughter
to Salome's bed.

In the mirror, I saw my eyes glitter.
I flung back the sticky red sheets,
and there, like I said – and ain't life a bitch –
was his head on a platter.

Eurydice

Girls, I was dead and down
in the Underworld, a shade,
a shadow of my former self, nowhen.
It was a place where language stopped,
a black full stop, a black hole
where words had to come to an end.
And end they did there,
last words,
famous or not.
It suited me down to the ground.

So imagine me there,
unavailable,
out of this world,
then picture my face in that place
of Eternal Repose,
in the one place you'd think a girl would be safe
from the kind of a man
who follows her round
writing poems,
hovers about
while she reads them,
calls her His Muse,
and once sulked for a night and a day
because she remarked on his weakness for abstract nouns.
Just picture my face
when I heard –
Ye Gods –
a familiar knock-knock-knock at Death's door.

Him.
Big O.
Larger than life.
With his lyre
and a poem to pitch, with me as the prize.

Things were different back then.
For the men, verse-wise,
Big O was the boy. Legendary.
The blurb on the back of his books claimed
that animals,
aardvark to zebra,
flocked to his side when he sang,
fish leapt in their shoals
at the sound of his voice,
even the mute, sullen stones at his feet
wept wee, silver tears.

Bollocks. (I'd done all the typing myself,
I should know.)
And given my time all over again,
rest assured that I'd rather speak for myself
than be Dearest, Beloved, Dark Lady, White Goddess,
        etc., etc.

In fact, girls, I'd rather be dead.

But the Gods are like publishers,
usually male,
and what you doubtless know of my tale
is the deal.

Orpheus strutted his stuff.

The bloodless ghosts were in tears.
Sisyphus sat on his rock for the first time in years.
Tantalus was permitted a couple of beers.

The woman in question could scarcely believe her ears.

Like it or not,
I must follow him back to our life –
Eurydice, Orpheus' wife –
to be trapped in his images, metaphors, similes,
octaves and sextets, quatrains and couplets,
elegies, limericks, villanelles,
histories, myths . . .

He'd been told that he mustn't look back
or turn round,
but walk steadily upwards,
myself right behind him,
out of the Underworld
into the upper air that for me was the past.
He'd been warned
that one look would lose me
for ever and ever.

So we walked, we walked.
Nobody talked.

Girls, forget what you've read.
It happened like this –
I did everything in my power
to make him look back.
What did I have to do, I said,
to make him see we were through?
I was dead. Deceased.
I was Resting in Peace. Passé. Late.
Past my sell-by date . . .
I stretched out my hand
to touch him once
on the back of his neck.
Please let me stay.
But already the light had saddened from purple to grey.

It was an uphill schlep
from death to life
and with every step
I willed him to turn.
I was thinking of filching the poem
out of his cloak,
when inspiration finally struck.
I stopped, thrilled.
He was a yard in front.
My voice shook when I spoke –
Orpheus, your poem's a masterpiece.
I'd love to hear it again . . .

He was smiling modestly
when he turned,
when he turned and he looked at me.

What else?
I noticed he hadn't shaved.
I waved once and was gone.

The dead are so talented.
The living walk by the edge of a vast lake
near the wise, drowned silence of the dead.

The Kray Sisters

There go the twins! geezers would say
when we walked down the frog and toad
in our Savile Row whistle and flutes, tailored
to flatter our thr'penny bits, which were big,
like our East End hearts. No one could tell us apart,
except when one twin wore glasses or shades
over two of our four mince pies. Oh, London, London,
London Town, made for a girl and her double
to swagger around; or be driven at speed
in the back of an Austin Princess, black,
up West to a club; to order up bubbly, the best,
in a bucket of ice. Garland singing that night. Nice.

Childhood. When we were God Forbids, we lived
with our grandmother – God Rest Her Soul – a tough
        suffragette
who'd knocked out a Grand National horse, name of
Ballytown Boy, with one punch, in front of the King,
for the cause. She was known round our manor thereafter
as Cannonball Vi. By the time we were six,
we were sat at her skirts, inhaling the juniper fumes
of her Vera Lynn; hearing the stories of Emmeline's Army
before and after the '14 war. Diamond ladies,
they were, those birds who fought for the Vote, salt
of the earth. And maybe this marked us for ever,
because of the loss of our mother, who died giving birth

to the pair of unusual us. Straight up, we knew,
even then, what we wanted to be; had, you could say,
a vocation. We wanted respect for the way
we entered a bar, or handled a car, or shrivelled
a hard-on with simply a menacing look, a threatening word
in a hairy ear, a knee in the orchestra stalls. Belles
of the balls. Queens of the Smoke. We dreamed it all,
trudging for miles, holding the hand of the past, learning
the map of the city under our feet; clocking the boozers,
back alleys, mews, the churches and bridges, the parks,
the Underground stations, the grand hotels where Vita and
      Violet,
pin-ups of ours, had given it wallop. We stared from
      Hungerford Bridge
as the lights of London tarted up the old Thames. All right,

we made our mistakes in those early years. We were soft
when we should have been hard; enrolled a few girls
in the firm who were well out of order – two of them
getting Engaged; a third sneaking back up the Mile End Road
every night to be some plonker's wife. Rule Number One –
A boyfriend's for Christmas, not just for life.
But we learned – and our twenty-first birthday saw us
      installed
in the first of our clubs, Ballbreakers, just off
Evering Road. The word got around and about
that any woman in trouble could come to the Krays,
no questions asked, for Protection. We'd soon earned the
      clout
and the dosh and respect for a move, Piccadilly way,

to a classier gaff – to the club at the heart of our legend,
Prickteasers. We admit, bang to rights, that the fruits
of feminism – fact – made us rich, feared, famous,
friends of the stars. Have a good butcher's at these –
there we for ever are in glamorous black-and-white,
assertively staring out next to Germaine, Bardot,
Twiggy and Lulu, Dusty and Yoko, Bassey, Babs,
Sandy, Diana Dors. And London was safer then
on account of us. Look at the letters we get –
*Dear Twins, them were the Good Old Days when you ruled
the streets. There was none of this mugging old ladies
or touching young girls.* We hear what's being said.

Remember us at our peak, in our prime, dressed to kill
and swaggering in to our club, stroke of twelve,
the evening we'd leaned on Sinatra to sing for free.
There was always a bit of a buzz when we entered, stopping
at favoured tables, giving a nod or a wink, buying someone
a drink, lighting a fag, lending an ear. That particular night
something electric, trembling, blue, crackled the air. Leave us
    both there,
spotlit, strong, at the top of our world, with Sinatra drawling
    And here's
a song for the twins, then opening her beautiful throat to take
it away. *These boots are made for walking, and that's
just what they'll do. One of these days these boots
are gonna walk all over you. Are you ready, boots? Start
    walkin'* . . .

Elvis's Twin Sister

Are you lonesome tonight? Do you miss me tonight?

Elvis is alive and she's female: Madonna

In the convent, y'all,
I tend the gardens,
watch things grow,
pray for the immortal soul
of rock 'n' roll.

They call me
Sister Presley here.
The Reverend Mother
digs the way I move my hips
just like my brother.

Gregorian chant
drifts out across the herbs,
Pascha nostrum immolatus est . . .
I wear a simple habit,
darkish hues,

a wimple with a novice-sewn
lace band, a rosary,
a chain of keys,
a pair of good and sturdy
blue suede shoes.

I think of it
as Graceland here,
a land of grace.
It puts my trademark slow lopsided smile
back on my face.

Lawdy.
I'm alive and well.
Long time since I walked
down Lonely Street
towards Heartbreak Hotel.

Pope Joan

After I learned to transubstantiate
unleavened bread
into the sacred host

and swung the burning frankincense
till blue-green snakes of smoke
coiled round the hem of my robe

and swayed through those fervent crowds,
high up in a papal chair,
blessing and blessing the air,

nearer to heaven
than cardinals, archbishops, bishops, priests,
being Vicar of Rome,

having made the Vatican my home,
like the best of men,
in nomine patris et filii et spiritus sancti amen,

but twice as virtuous as them,
I came to believe
that I did not believe a word,

so I tell you now,
daughters or brides of the Lord,
that the closest I felt

to the power of God
was the sense of a hand
lifting me, flinging me down,

lifting me, flinging me down,
as my baby pushed out
from between my legs

where I lay in the road
in my miracle,
not a man or a pope at all.

Penelope

At first, I looked along the road
hoping to see him saunter home
among the olive trees,
a whistle for the dog
who mourned him with his warm head on my knees.
Six months of this
and then I noticed that whole days had passed
without my noticing.
I sorted cloth and scissors, needle, thread,

thinking to amuse myself,
but found a lifetime's industry instead.
I sewed a girl
under a single star – cross-stitch, silver silk –
running after childhood's bouncing ball.
I chose between three greens for the grass;
a smoky pink, a shadow's grey
to show a snapdragon gargling a bee.
I threaded walnut brown for a tree,

my thimble like an acorn
pushing up through umber soil.
Beneath the shade
I wrapped a maiden in a deep embrace
with heroism's boy
and lost myself completely
in a wild embroidery of love, lust, loss, lessons learnt;
then watched him sail away
into the loose gold stitching of the sun.

And when the others came to take his place,
disturb my peace,
I played for time.
I wore a widow's face, kept my head down,
did my work by day, at night unpicked it.
I knew which hour of the dark the moon
would start to fray,
I stitched it.
Grey threads and brown

pursued my needle's leaping fish
to form a river that would never reach the sea.
I tricked it. I was picking out
the smile of a woman at the centre
of this world, self-contained, absorbed, content,
most certainly not waiting,
when I heard a far-too-late familiar tread outside the door.
I licked my scarlet thread
and aimed it surely at the middle of the needle's eye once
        more.

Mrs Beast

These myths going round, these legends, fairytales,
I'll put them straight; so when you stare
into my face – Helen's face, Cleopatra's,
Queen of Sheba's, Juliet's – then, deeper,
gaze into my eyes – Nefertiti's, Mona Lisa's,
Garbo's eyes – think again. The Little Mermaid slit
her shining, silver tail in two, rubbed salt
into that stinking wound, got up and walked,
in agony, in fishnet tights, stood up and smiled, waltzed,
all for a Prince, a pretty boy, a charming one
who'd dump her in the end, chuck her, throw her overboard.
I could have told her – look, love, I should know,
they're bastards when they're Princes.
What you want to do is find yourself a Beast. The sex

is better. Myself, I came to the House of the Beast
no longer a girl, knowing my own mind,
my own gold stashed in the bank,
my own black horse at the gates
ready to carry me off at one wrong word,
one false move, one dirty look.
But the Beast fell to his knees at the door
to kiss my glove with his mongrel lips – good –
showed by the tears in his bloodshot eyes
that he knew he was blessed – better –
didn't try to conceal his erection,
size of a mule's – best. And the Beast
watched me open, decant and quaff
a bottle of Château Margaux '54,
the year of my birth, before he lifted a paw.

I'll tell you more. Stripped of his muslin shirt
and his corduroys, he steamed in his pelt,
ugly as sin. He had the grunts, the groans, the yelps,
the breath of a goat. I had the language, girls.
The lady says Do this. Harder. The lady says
Do that. Faster. The lady says That's not where I meant.
At last it all made sense. The pig in my bed
was *invited*. And if his snout and trotters fouled
my damask sheets, why, then, he'd wash them. Twice.
Meantime, here was his horrid leather tongue
to scour in between my toes. Here
were his hooked and yellowy claws to pick my nose,
if I wanted that. Or to scratch my back
till it bled. Here was his bullock's head
to sing off-key all night where I couldn't hear.
Here was a bit of him like a horse, a ram,
an ape, a wolf, a dog, a donkey, dragon, dinosaur.

Need I say more? On my Poker nights, the Beast
kept out of sight. We were a hard school, tough as fuck,
all of us beautiful and rich – the Woman
who Married a Minotaur, Goldilocks, the Bride
of the Bearded Lesbian, Frau Yellow Dwarf, et Moi.
I watched those wonderful women shuffle and deal –
Five and Seven Card Stud, Sidewinder, Hold 'Em, Draw –

I watched them bet and raise and call. One night,
a head-to-head between Frau Yellow Dwarf and Bearded's
       Bride
was over the biggest pot I'd seen in my puff.
The Frau had the Queen of Clubs on the baize
and Bearded the Queen of Spades. Final card. Queen each.
Frau Yellow raised. Bearded raised. Goldilocks' eyes
were glued to the pot as though porridge bubbled there.
The Minotaur's wife lit a stinking cheroot. Me,
I noticed the Frau's hand shook as she placed her chips.
Bearded raised her a final time, then stared,
stared so hard you felt your dress would melt
if she blinked. I held my breath. Frau Yellow
swallowed hard, then called. Sure enough, Bearded flipped
her Aces over; diamonds, hearts, the pubic Ace of Spades.
And that was a lesson learnt by all of us –
the drop-dead gorgeous Bride of the Bearded Lesbian didn't
       bluff.

But behind each player stood a line of ghosts
unable to win. Eve. Ashputtel. Marilyn Monroe.
Rapunzel slashing wildly at her hair.
Bessie Smith unloved and down and out.
Bluebeard's wives, Henry VIII's, Snow White
cursing the day she left the seven dwarfs, Diana,
Princess of Wales. The sheepish Beast came in
with a tray of schnapps at the end of the game
and we stood for the toast – *Fay Wray* –
then tossed our fiery drinks to the back of our crimson
       throats.
Bad girls. Serious ladies. Mourning our dead.

So I was hard on the Beast, win or lose,
when I got upstairs, those tragic girls in my head,
turfing him out of bed; standing alone
on the balcony, the night so cold I could taste the stars
on the tip of my tongue. And I made a prayer –
thumbing my pearls, the tears of Mary, one by one,
like a rosary – words for the lost, the captive beautiful,
the wives, those less fortunate than we.
The moon was a hand-mirror breathed on by a Queen.
My breath was a chiffon scarf for an elegant ghost.
I turned to go back inside. Bring me the Beast for the night.
Bring me the wine-cellar key. Let the less-loving one be me.

Demeter

Where I lived – winter and hard earth.
I sat in my cold stone room
choosing tough words, granite, flint,

to break the ice. My broken heart –
I tried that, but it skimmed,
flat, over the frozen lake.

She came from a long, long way,
but I saw her at last, walking,
my daughter, my girl, across the fields,

in bare feet, bringing all spring's flowers
to her mother's house. I swear
the air softened and warmed as she moved,

the blue sky smiling, none too soon,
with the small shy mouth of a new moon.

Afterword

What I wanted to do in the book was to look at all the stories –
fairy tales, myths, stories from history, film and popular music or
whatever, stories of heroes or villains which had informed me as a
writer, part of my cultural ancestry. I wanted to celebrate them, in
a way, but also find a truth which hadn't been amplified previously.
The way I wanted to do that was to find a female perspective on
the character, and I did that by finding a personal connection with
the fairy tale, myth, piece of cinema, etc., so that although I'm
wearing the mask of Queen Herod or Mrs Beast I'm not discon-
nected from my own place, my own life. It might be that it is
autobiographical in the sense that it is true to my imaginative life
or my emotional life but not necessarily true to the actual details
of my life. At a later stage, I ordered the poems in a loose chrono-
logical movement. We start with 'Little Red Cap' which is about a
young girl becoming a poet and end with 'Demeter' which is about
a woman becoming a mother, so that it follows the arc of my own
life in some ways.

What you can do as a poet is take on a story and make it new.
Dramatists do this all the time. One of the poems in the book is
'Pygmalion', which has been used as a template by writers from
George Bernard Shaw to Willy Russell in *Educating Rita*; old
stories which are made fresh.

Therefore the original concept was to take stories I'd been
formed by, from childhood. In my particular case I had a Catholic
upbringing, I went to a Catholic primary school and then a
convent school, so stories from the Bible, particularly the New
Testament, were part of my background on a daily basis; there
was church more than once a week, confession and communion
and that sort of thing, and my brothers were altar boys. These
stories are very close to me, and I didn't just think 'one from the
Bible, one from Shakespeare'. These tales were just there in the way

in which family stories and family mythology are always there. I completed thirty poems but there could have been a lot more.

For me these poems are a celebration really – of language, relationships, being human. To write about anything at all, even if you're critical of your subject, is to celebrate, is to make something, to add something to the world. It's a giving act. I never felt, in the writing of the *World's Wife* poems, that the main endeavour was to have a go at certain aspects of maleness, although I can see that that's part of what comes out of the content. My aim was to find hidden truths or fresh, female ways of looking at familiar things.

I didn't want every woman in the book to be better than the men. That wasn't my agenda, so I wanted to look at unpleasant aspects of being female as well as look at ways of being male. I wanted to look at ways of being human really. It just so happens that the stories that I grew up with feature men – Faust, Midas, Tiresias, Pilate, King Herod – what I've tried to do is put some female into it. I wasn't trying to attack the male, but put the female into it, into the story.

With all of them, I'm looking at the story, and I'm thinking the events are the same but I might change the interpretation of events. And of course the main change is from male to female views of things: that's what you say, but what does she say? And in any situation there'll be a different explanation of events. In that sense, although the book has been called a feminist manifesto, and I am feminist and it is feminist, my aim was larger than that – I wanted to be able to expand the stories and to bring in extra layers of truth. I wanted to add, and not take away from the originals.

Carol Ann Duffy
Taken from an interview with Barry Wood,
2005, for *Sheer Poetry*